Create your dream house and garden

Create your dream house and garden

52 brilliant little ideas for big home improvements

J Cook, M Hillsdon,
A Marsden & L O'Prey

brilliantideas

CAREFUL NOW

Follow the tips in this book
and you could find yourself
the proud owner of a beautiful
home. Do be careful though –
if you're planning any major
work make sure you call in
the professionals (builders,
plumbers, architects, those
sorts of people). And don't
come crying to us if you try to
do it all yourself and end up
living in a building site.

First published in 2008 by
The Infinite Ideas Company Limited
36 St Giles
Oxford
OX1 3LD
United Kingdom
www.infideas.com

A CIP catalogue record for this book is available from the
British Library

ISBN 978-1-905940-40-0

Designed and typeset by Baseline Arts Ltd, Oxford
Printed in China

Brilliant ideas

Introduction

Set aside all the practical reasons why you
have a home – a roof over your head, a place
to sleep, somewhere to eat, storage for all your
possessions, a garden to relax in – and
consider just one thing: do you love being there?

Does your garden intrigue you but terrify you at the same time? You
love the idea of growing your own vegetables but worry about using
chemicals to keep the pests off. And as much as you love them, why
exactly do some clematis insist on having their roots in the shade?
Back inside, does the combination of colours, the choice of
furniture, the use of materials and the way it's been laid out fit
perfectly with your tastes and lifestyle?

If you find yourself thinking that this is not entirely the case, then
maybe it's time to make some changes. Here's where this book steps
in. There are guidelines that you can follow and advice that makes
great sense and while we're not big fans of rules, some can be
applied to tackling the design of your home and garden (but don't
feel that you always have to stick to them rigidly). Interpret them in
your own way and for your specific situation.

You can seek the advice of professional designers and they will probably do a magnificent job. But wouldn't it be more fun and give you greater satisfaction if you knew that the inspiration and execution were all your own? This book will help you make the best decisions about how to make your home and garden outstanding. You may agree with some of the ideas and you may find others just don't fit with your own perception of what works. This book sets out to inspire rather than lay down the law, so please use it as a guide and not a set of rules. It will hopefully result in you understanding much more about the spaces in which you live.

And don't for get it's all intended to be enjoyable. Gardening and decorating may be hard work but they should be a labour of love. We hope this book helps you to create your perfect space.

1. Did the earth move?

Get to know your soil and you can add the right stuff to improve it, and grow the types of plants that will enjoy it.

To find the pH of your soil you need a soil-testing kit, available at any garden centre. It pays to take three or four samples from the outer edges of the garden as you may have more than one soil type, each favouring different plants and treatments. The test will show whether your samples are acidic (below 7), neutral (7) or alkaline (above 7). Most garden plants favour soil that is slightly acidic at 6.5, but there's still a good selection of plants for neutral and alkaline soils.

With your pH sorted, discovering your soil type is even easier. Just pick some up. If it's tightly packed, squeezes into a sticky ball and hangs about on your boots – it's clay. If it feels gritty, and water runs through it easily – it's sandy. If you discover the white cliffs of Dover under the surface – it's chalk.

Clay soil is hard to work. It's wet and cloggy in winter and bakes rock hard in a dry spell. But it is full of good things and the nutrients your plants need to grow, so don't despair. You do need to improve its drainage though, so mix in some horticultural grit or coarse sand when planting. Clay soil is usually neutral to acidic too so add lime – ground down calcium – especially if you're growing brassicas. Turn unplanted ground over in the autumn and leave the frost to break up the big lumps.

Success on sand will depend on how you can help the soil hang on to food and moisture. Adding in compost will help retain water and fertiliser long enough for it to do some good. But this will need to become a regular chore so you may wish to just focus on parts of the garden where you are growing hungry, thirsty plants such as the veg.

Chalky soil can be stony, or sticky and thin, but it's well-drained and you can work on it most of the year. Bulk it up by adding organic matter. Horse manure, which tends to be full of straw, is good for sticky chalk. As it breaks down relatively quickly, spread it on the surface and leave the earthworms to do their bit. Dig in any left over straw in the spring.

2. Wood looks

From bare boards to the finest finishes, choose wood for your floors.

There is something very appealing about walking into a room with bare boards. It has a pared down simplicity that can make other more exotic options seem a little extravagant. There's a rich variety of looks that are available to you if you opt for wood.

Wood works in every setting. It is cooler than carpet but much warmer than stone, makes the perfect background for rugs and will work with virtually any colour scheme. In fact if you can decide on nothing other than a wooden floor as part of your decorating scheme for a room, then at least you can be assured that you have made an excellent first step in the planning process.

Age old
Old wood floors should be kept where possible. Sanding, stripping and finishing is within most people's range of expertise even if these jobs are time consuming and very messy. If you have just plain boards, then it is quite straightforward, however if you discover that

you have parquet you need to approach it with a little more care.
Any loose blocks, for example, should be refitted before you make
any attempt to renovate the actual surface of the wood.

Modern choices
Here are two of the most popular choices for a wood floor:
- Veneered or laminate flooring can be pre-assembled in long
  strips ready to clip together. It comes in several different grades
  and is impact- and scratch-resistant.
- Hardwood floor can come in either square-edge or tongue-and-
  groove planks and can be supplied to you either finished or
  unfinished. It also comes in a range of different patterns,
  including maple, ash, cherry, oak and beech.

If you want a new wood floor, then for the ultimate in durability
choose a solid hardwood floor: it'll gain character with age and will
last for a decade or two. This type of flooring is at the top of the
price range. For less expensive options consider laminate strips,
many of which can be laid by even an incompetent DIYer. Bear in
mind that laminate flooring may have only the thinnest of veneers
on top of the wood facing and it won't be as durable as some of the
more expensive options.

3. Top seed

Every seed is a gardening miracle, a small, dried out husk that a few months after planting bursts into flower and brings new life to the garden.

The first rule of successful sowing is to read the packet! It should tell you all you need to know. For instance, do your seeds need soaking before you plant them? This can soften the outer husks or remove chemicals that prevent them from germinating. Are they suitable for sowing in trays or pots, or should you sow them directly into the ground?

While the professionals use all kinds of weird and wonderful 'growing' mediums such as rock-wool, a good quality seed compost is probably best for the amateur. Try to get one that contains sterilised loam and a peat substitute, which will be finer and more moisture retentive than either a general purpose compost or home grown humus, which will be too rich for the seeds.

As a rule of thumb, the larger the seed the easier it is to grow. Big seeds like lupins and sweet peas are best sown individually in pots, which means they can develop a good strong root system before you disturb them and plant them out. Or better still in this environmentally conscious age, why not use a biodegradable pot. Used for larger seeds, you can miss out the pricking out stage and just plant the whole thing, pot and all, into the ground.

As they develop, your seeds will need differing levels of light, warmth, air and moisture and, once that shoot appears, nutrients as well. Read up on what you have to do so that you aren't caught on the hop.

As a general rule, the trick is to make sure the compost is damp but not waterlogged; the atmosphere is humid but not dripping. A watering can with a fine rose will help and you can improve the overall drainage by part filling the bottom of the pots with gravel.

Next you need to prick them out by gently prising out each seedling by its leaves (not the stalk) using a dibber, and move it on to a pot of its own, before growing them on, hardening them off, and planting them out. Then you can enjoy them. Nobody said it was going to be easy!

4. The pattern rules

Using patterns is a great way of brightening a colour scheme and adding visual excitement and interest to a space, but it just needs handling with some care to make combinations work.

Tartan, for example, immediately makes a room feel warm and cosy. It can be used to add a quirky touch to townhouses.

Simple floral patterns suggest spring. They are optimists in the fabric family symptomatic of new starts and fresh beginnings. Walk into a room where these designs have been used and even the most dedicated of minimalists will enjoy a lift to their spirit.

Stripes have the effect of making a space seem quite 'grown up'. There is something about the regular nature of this pattern that makes people sit with straight backs and sip their tea without slopping it into the saucer. It has a formal quality to it that can be usefully employed in period houses.

Geometrics could be seen as the juveniles in the group. Squares, circles and squiggly shapes evoke a mood of careless enjoyment. Slightly cheeky and reminiscent of the 50s, 60s and 70s when women were liberated and music became rock and roll, they are perfect for modern flats and new conversions.

Here are a few ideas to help you work with pattern...

- Avoid using lots of tiny motifs in the same space – it will look much too busy.
- Think about using large designs with care: if the motif on a wallpaper is very big, how many complete designs will fit in to the drop on the wall – if you can only see one or two, is it going to work?
- Where your walls are plain, introduce patterns on cushion covers or lampshades. If your furniture is all relatively plain, use a patterned paint effect or wallpaper on the walls.
- Don't mix two very different styles – avoid teaming Chinese-influenced oriental designs and an African-style ethnic pattern in the same room, for example.

Make your colour choices with care when you mix up different patterns and you can create quite spectacular effects in a room.

5. Free plants

When taking cuttings, different plants respond to different methods but here are some general rules.

- Softwood cuttings (taken from the top of the stem) work for perennials and most shrubs, and should be taken in spring. The cutting needs to be up to 7cm long. Cut just before a leaf node (the bit where the leaves form) and remove the lower leaves. Root these cuttings first in a jar of water and move to small pots of compost once the roots have formed.
- Semi-ripe cuttings (using wood that is soft at the top and firmer at the base) for trees, shrubs and roses, should be taken in mid-to-late summer. Ease a shoot, about 12cm long, from the plant so that a 'heel' of the parent plant remains attached. Leave the top foliage on and put the bare part into the compost. Place several cuttings into one pot, moving each onto individual pots once a good root has formed.
- Hard wood (strong, hard stems from the current year's growth, with soft top removed) for shrubs and some fruits, taken between mid-autumn and early winter. Take pencil thick cuttings, trim to 20cm long, making a straight cut at the bottom,

just below a leaf node, and a slanted cut at the top, above a leaf node. Place cuttings in an outside trench or potted in cold frame and leave for up to a year.

- Root cuttings, taken from the roots of trees, shrubs or herbaceous plants, should be taken when the plant is dormant in the autumn. Unearth some of the root and remove a piece about the width of a pencil and as long as possible. Cut this into pieces of at least 5cm. To ensure you plant them the right way up, cut the end that was severed from the plant straight, the other end at an angle. Place them in a pot with the straight end showing just above the surface, cover with 1cm of sharp sand and leave out until the spring

- Leaf cuttings, from healthy fully developed leaves, work especially well with begonias and African violets. Either carefully remove the whole leaf, complete with stalk, and inset into a shallow hole in a pot of compost, or nick the underside veins of a leaf and lay it topside up on the compost surface. Cut sword like leaves into sections of 5cm long and inset each upright into the compost. Once plantlets develop pot them on.

6. Get organised

Try a bit of well-planned storage in your home and you'll be amazed how pleased you are with the results.

The key to good storage is to consider the room first and the storage second. Don't just go out and buy a cupboard that you think might 'fit in somewhere'. You want to be clear about the room it will work in, the purpose it will serve, and whether it is going to offer the maximum possible storage space for the room. Approach it room-by-room, as your requirements for the lounge are very different to your needs in the study. Apply a critical eye to each room, breaking down your possessions into groups. Which items need to be within easy and accessible reach? Are there certain things, which only get occasional use? Most importantly, is there anything that you can get rid of? Also apply a bit of lateral thinking. Not all storage has to be positioned on the floor and sometimes the best solutions are concealed from the eye.

Concealed storage has real appeal; a table with drawers hidden underneath or it a footstool with space under the lid. The more items like this that you can find, the less you will need to rely on cupboards that take up valuable floor space. Of course there are some items that you want to see and have easy access to, like books.

Consider if there are any wasted spaces in the house where you might put a bookshelf – the landing is a often an area that is left clear of any furniture but if you think about it, might there be room for a full-height set of bookshelves?

Every hall should have somewhere to deposit coats and shoes (umbrellas, school bags and gym kits too). Look for a unit that has a mirror at the front and shelves concealed behind.

The bathroom can be a real challenge if you have a fairly small room. There are units available that fit over the top of the toilet providing shelves or a cabinet above your head for keeping all your necessary bits and pieces.

The secret of good storage is adaptability and versatility, so spend time researching dual-purpose pieces and practical items that fulfil all of your needs.

7. Design without despair

You don't need a degree in landscape architecture to give shape to your garden – just a bit of inspiration, a rudimentary knowledge and plenty of elbow grease.

From the start it pays to have some vision or picture of how things are going to look when you're finished. You need to get a feel for the site, thinking about what could go where and then working out whether it really should. Where are the garden's sunny spots? Where's the shade? Does anywhere tend to get waterlogged?

The first essential is to establish which direction your garden faces. On a suitable day follow the path of the sun across your garden noting the variations in light and shade, because while you may be basking in the reflected glory of a south facing plot, it could sit under the canopy of the neighbour's spreading chestnut tree for most of the day.

OK, now the fun really starts. Armed with small stakes or pegs mark out certain areas, such as the herbaceous border, rose bed and vegetable patch. A hosepipe is a great help in doing this, as being both light and flexible, it will give you an immediate outline on which you can pass judgment.

At this stage, don't even think about any permanent structures like brick walls – their role and positioning will become more obvious as the rest of the garden takes shape. Shifting a few barrow loads of misplaced soil is one thing – reconstructing a wall or concrete path is another.

If you want a water feature, fine, but remember it doesn't have to be a lake. You could always confine yourself to a mini fountain or birdbath.

No matter how small your garden, you can still make use of existing rises and falls too, or create new and different levels. They help give the impression of more space and give you the opportunity to make a new patio or seating area. The idea should be to create mystery! Try not to open everything up at once. Add fences, a winding path, a trellis or pergola smothered in climbers, which will tempt your visitors to find out what's going on behind.

8. Room at the top

**There's a great way to avoid moving house
if your reason for leaving is because you
have outgrown your home – make use of
the space at the top of the house.**

A loft conversion is the most sensible way of getting an extra room
(well that and adding on a conservatory, but you may well have done
that already).

First, ask yourself some basic questions...

■ What is your budget?
■ How will the room be used?
■ Where are you going to put the extra staircase that you will need?
■ How are you going to lay out the space to accommodate the
  slopes and awkward shapes that the roof creates?

Knowing your budget is vital (not just for the building work but also
the furnishing and decoration) because you need to decide whether
you can afford a dormer window which projects to the outside to
form a full-height area in the loft with a vertical window or whether

you will have to settle for a cheaper roof window which is set into the slope of the roof. Planning regulations in your area may also affect this choice.

You need to have a good idea of the ultimate use of the space because if it is going to be an office you'll need a telephone point, lots of electrical sockets for all of your computer kit, and light fittings to illuminate the work area. Consider up-lighters rather than a pendant fitting because they will throw light up towards what will probably be a reasonably low ceiling. Alternatively halogen spots set into the ceiling are a good option.

The position of the staircase is important because you are going to have to lose space from somewhere on the floor below. If you are worried about it encroaching on a bedroom, then maybe think about a spiral staircase.

If you can afford it, think about including built-in storage in the room. It will work around the slopes of the ceiling making the maximum use of any awkward areas in the room. Because the room that the conversion creates is unlikely to be huge, you want to avoid cluttering it up with lots of different pieces of freestanding furniture wherever possible.

9. Heap it on

A garden without a compost heap is like a car without an engine – it ain't going anywhere.

The first rule of composting is to know what goes on the heap and what goes on the fire. For starters, perennial weeds and anything diseased should be burnt, while anything too woody, unless finely shredded, should be bagged up and taken to the local tip. And only add cooked foodstuffs if you want to attract a family of rats to your garden.

Now for the good bits. Kitchen waste is perfect and if you're serious about this set up a separate bin for your peelings and pods. The autumn clear up, particularly of the herbaceous borders, will also give you plenty of raw material.

Grass cuttings are a permanent source of controversy. Use them by all means but layer them between other fibrous material, to avoid black, nourishment free slurry. Dead leaves can also be tricky if just dumped on a heap. But they are worth persevering with, so store them separately in punctured plastic bags or better still in chicken wire cages. They will compost, but in years rather than months.

The other perennial question is whether a compost heap should be wet or dry. The advice is neither. Yes, it needs to be covered with something like an old piece of carpet, as this helps build up the heat and accelerate decomposition. But it pays to leave it exposed occasionally to rain, as it shouldn't be allowed to dry out.

The ultimate prize is horse or cow manure, and you'll be surprised how easy it is to get hold of the stuff, even if you live in town, with its riding schools and city farms. However don't be tempted to spread fresh manure as this will scorch your plants. Leave it for at least six months, until it no longer resembles dung and is more like crumbly soil.

In an ideal world you need three bins. Leave a full bin for approximately three months before turning it into the next one. Then repeat the process and you should achieve the ultimate crumbly brown compost within six to nine months.

10. A taste for tiles

Resistant to dirt and easy to clean, tiles make a logical choice for rooms that receive a lot of wear and tear.

If you think about the volume of water that gets splashed around in the bathroom, the amount of steam in the kitchen, and the rain and dirt that flies around in a hallway, it becomes obvious why tiles are a good choice for the walls.

Thinking about your kitchen, here are some elements that might influence your choice:

- How much wall space are you looking to cover with the tiles? If you have wall-mounted cabinets, then you may only have a small area to tile and can afford to choose more expensive hand-made tiles over mass-produced ceramic designs.

- Is there a space that you want to fill with a panel or mural of tiles? There is a huge variety of designs that can be bought off the shelf. These can be set on the wall in the middle of plain tiles or surrounded with a contrasting colour to frame the view.

- Do you want to combine mostly plain tiles with just a scattering of patterned ones? A few hand-painted delft tiles might look perfect introduced at random in a rustic country kitchen, while metallic abstract designs could be a way to add an intriguing detail in a modern room.

In the bathroom you are likely to be covering large areas so cost is much more of a consideration.

- Budget to cover the largest area possible. It makes cleaning and maintaining the bathroom so much easier if all the walls are tiled.
- Do you have a separate shower area that needs completely tiling? If that cuts into your budget, then limit yourself to a tiled splashback above the sink. Stand up in your bath and tile to the height of your shoulders around that area. That should be sufficient to protect the wall from even the most vigorous of splashing bathers.
- Have you considered mosaic tiles in the bathroom? These look absolutely stunning whether they are in bright colours or natural shades. Bright Mediterranean blue mosaics have a visual impact that is unrivalled in the tile world.

11. Tools of the trade

If there's one aspect of gardening where you mustn't skimp, it is choosing the right selection of tools.

First and foremost buy the best spade on the market. It should be made of stainless steel – rust free, easy to clean and will slide through even the stickiest soils.

Take care too over your second in command, the garden fork. Buy a cheap one and the tines will twist or the shaft split at the first sign of hard work. The choice of handle and how the stem is secured to the prongs, are most important. Select the size you feel comfortable with, one that will suit the jobs you have in mind – a heavy duty fork for digging and turning the compost heap or a smaller border fork for areas full of plants.

But pride of place goes to three unlikely and certainly unheralded tools: the pickaxe, the builder's barrow and the sack truck. The pickaxe has many obvious uses such as lifting stones or breaking heavy, compacted soil. But what about getting under obstinate tree roots, moving shrubs and digging holes for fence posts?

Wheelbarrows that are based on the builder's barrow design have a strong but light frame with comfortably spaced handles, ample capacity in a galvanised steel bin, a pneumatic tyre and a tipping bar. Wooden barrows may win in the aesthetics stakes but can be heavy enough to lift even when empty. As for plastic versions, they're fine if your garden waste is confined to vegetation but no good for the rough stuff.

A sack truck is another must. Why risk your back heaving around bags of compost, heavy stones, pots and containers, when you can slide a sack truck underneath and wheel it along like a doll's pram? Its versatility will amaze you.

A good pair of secateurs is vital. Buy the best, look after them and you'll be well rewarded. But only use them for the job for which they were intended – which is cutting stems no more that 2cm thick. Anything bigger, and you'll just blunt them.
Clean your tools regularly but, come the end of the autumn, clean, oil and – where appropriate – sharpen them, because as all responsible gardeners know, garden tools are for life, not just for Christmas.

12. Flatter your floors

**The beauty of rugs is their versatility.
They can be used to bring colour or a
change of texture to a room, or
sometimes they are there to define a
particular space.**

If you have a dining area at the end of the lounge, putting a rug
down in that space creates the visual illusion of a different area. If
you have an enormous lounge or live in a studio-style space with no
dividing walls, use a rug to mark out different territories. Place one
in the middle of a group of chairs and a sofa and it draws everyone
into that space. Put one down in between the kitchen and the
seating area and it breaks up that part of the room and emphasises
the fact that there are two distinct zones in use.

The successful positioning of rugs relies on drawing the eye to a
particular space. This might suggest that the rug needs to be
brightly coloured or boldly patterned, but that isn't the case. The
mere fact that it sits proud of the floor beneath is enough to work
its magic. You can use a pale-coloured rug on top of a natural wood
floor and still achieve your aim, but if it has a border in a contrasting
colour that may help.

If you have any lingering doubts about rugs, then consider the following scenarios:

- You have a wood floor in the lounge, all the seats are taken but you would like some people to be able to sit on the floor: a thick rug provides some cushioning for their bottoms.
- The colour scheme in your bedroom is fairly neutral but you are aware that a subtle touch of colour would add the finishing touch: a striped cotton rug, laid beside the bed, will introduce a bit of pattern to the room.
- The stone floor in the hall is very practical but it is also extremely cold: a rug placed away from the entrance but running down the rest of the room is much more inviting to new arrivals.

If you want a subtle way of adding warmth, comfort and a touch of colour or pattern to a room, you can look to rugs to provide a solution.

13. Grass roots

With a bit of seasonal savvy you can transform rough turf into something that resembles centre court at Wimbledon.

The first step is to know when and how to cut your grass. Regular cutting helps to invigorate the growing tips so, for this reason, mowing the lawn should be seen as a year round job – including winter, when just a couple of cuts can make all the difference come spring. There's more to master mowing than meets the eye. Cut it too short, and the grass won't get enough water, too long, and it will bend over and stop new shoots from getting any sun. Consistency is the key. If you do let the lawn get too long then don't cut it right back in one go, as this will cause scalping. As a general rule never remove more than one third of the leaf in any single mowing.

Watering is as crucial as it is easy to overlook. Hose pipe bans permitting, don't leave it too late to give your lawn a good soaking as turf that's already turned yellow or brown is unlikely to be revived.

For larger, bald patches turfing may be more suitable, and is quicker than reseeding but more expensive. For reseeding, fork the whole area, re-level the soil, and sow at the full recommended rate. Easy!

As for grass type – seed or turf – the current vogue is for dwarf perennial rye, which offers all the traditional toughness of rye but the added attraction of ornamental leaves. For a more delicate look you may want to look into clump-forming grasses such as fescue or bent. It's true that their resistance to constant wear and tear, and to disease, is limited, but on the other hand you can cheer yourself up with a chuckle over their names.

It's also important to aerate an established lawn by forking it in both spring and autumn. This helps to alleviate compaction and helps drainage, but it can be an arduous task. Alternatives include mechanical aerators which you can hire, or specially spiked overshoes which do the job as you simply walk up and down. Drainage can be further improved by applying a top dressing of six parts sand to three parts soil and one part peat substitute. This can then be brushed into the holes.

14. Compact and bijoux

Simple solutions for pocket-sized spaces.

In any situation where your floor space is limited you need to decorate and design it so that the area seems larger than it is. In the first place, choose a light colour to paint your walls. In the second place choose a light colour to decorate your ceiling. In the third place choose a light-coloured flooring. (You will bring in other details later so that this isn't as bland as it sounds.)

Now let's be realistic. You can't have a massive sofa, or a king-sized bed. Apart from the style issues that need to be considered, they probably won't go up the stairs or get through the door. When you buy furniture for small spaces work on the principle that, where possible, you want to get two uses out of one item. A coffee table doubles up as a dining table if you have floor cushions to sit on while you eat, a storage chest functions as extra seating when covered with lovely blankets or throws, and a set of shelves can also become a room divider. Once you start to work on this principle you'll find your own ways to adapt things in your home.

Colour is a useful tool in defining spaces. Variations on the walls and in the floor can be a great way to signpost a change of use. While everything should be kept light, you can still use a slightly darker paint in two different spaces. If your kitchen is pure white, then decorate the adjacent designated dining area in a shade of stone. And you can change the flooring – if the lounge area in a studio is covered in wood laminate, then choose seagrass to cover the space that you use as a study.

Consider investing in vertical blinds or sliding panels to screen off spaces. These can be fitted to run from floor to ceiling and are easily pulled out of the way when you want to be open plan, and drawn back into place when you wish to separate off your sleeping area for example.

With clever use of colour and careful planning, even the smallest space works as a fully functioning home.

15. Slugging it out

**There's more than one way to defeat the
gardener's number one foe.**

Your garden is likely to be home to several
kinds of slugs and snails, but it's the grey field slug that does most
damage, closely followed by the chestnut and garden slugs. And
while the large black ones may be the easiest to pick off, they
probably do less damage than the other three. Snails are said to be
less destructive, particularly the banded ones, although large, grey
common garden snails, and smaller strawberry snails, with their
flattened shell, have voracious appetites.

The jury is still out on whether slug pellets really do harm wildlife
by killing off the thrushes and frogs that eat the poisonous cadavers.
But until there's concrete evidence to the contrary, surely it makes
sense to use a more wildlife-friendly aluminium sulphate based
pellet instead.

Also effective are beer traps, sunk into the ground and filled with
your least favourite brew. Half a grapefruit does just as well but
these devices are indiscriminate and will take out ground beetles
too, an important slug predator. Other tips include keeping your

garden free of leaf litter and plant debris, which gives the slugs somewhere to chill out during the day. Weeds, especially dandelions, are also believed to entice slugs away from your blooms.

The best form of defence is, of course, attack and although pricey, nematodes certainly work. These naturally occurring parasites eat the slugs and you can boost the numbers in the soil by mixing a packet of the microscopic bugs with water and applying as per the instructions. You'll soon notice a lot less devastation in your borders.

Be aware that nature maintains a certain number of snails in any one garden, so there's always a clutch of baby monsters waiting to take the place of the ones you remove. For a longer-term approach, try encouraging some allies into the garden. A pond will enhance the frog population, while a pellet-free garden is more likely to attract nesting birds. And if you don't feed birds after June, they'll be more likely to seek out the pests in your garden instead.

A cool, damp place, such as the bottom of a stone wall or behind a water butt will encourage toads to set up residence, and if you live near water, then encourage ducks and moorhens into the garden – both thrive on slugs.

16. Lounging around

Design your living room for each and every situation.

If you put together the 'as near perfect as you can' living room, you have achieved a level of success in interior design for which you can be truly proud. It means that you have understood the principles of laying out a room, embraced the idea that a space works on many levels, and chosen furniture to fulfil a whole range of requirements.

Supplement your sofa with one or two armchairs so that should you wish to sprawl out, then everyone else can relax too. If you bring in a pouffe and some floor cushions other people can put their feet up or relax on the floor. Look through any contemporary mail order catalogue and you'll find wool-, felt- and suede-covered stools that are a far cry from the designs available to our parents' generation.

Now, what about reading and watching the television? You might be thinking that they require nothing special, but have you got your lights positioned so that there is no glare on the screen and so that you aren't going to strain your eyes? A lamp that can be moved around to accommodate your activities is an essential piece of kit in the lounge. Without it you have to rely on overhead or wall lights and these can never be positioned perfectly to suit every activity.

Next, have you got a table close to hand? Whether it's a coffee table that stays in one place or part of a nest of three that you pull out and use according to your needs, you want somewhere that you can set down the remote control or pile up the numerous sections of the weekend papers.

Any space that accommodates all of these activities also has a responsibility to cope with the associated flotsam and jetsam. There will be books that need a home and CDs and DVDs that you have got to store somewhere. If you have a space either side of a chimneybreast then you have the perfect place for housing custom-built shelving. A recess created by the positioning of a dividing wall can serve the same purpose. Alternatively, buy a freestanding unit but make sure that you can adjust the height of the shelves.

Designing a practical lounge takes some planning, but once the pieces are in place you'll be glad that you spent the time getting it right.

17. Growing under glass

Whether you're pottering in a top-of-the-range greenhouse or hunched over a cold frame, growing under glass can deliver miraculous results.

If you're time-poor investing in a free standing greenhouse with all its accessories might be a waste. Instead think about a cold frame or mini lean-to greenhouses which are cheaper and less demanding. These can still give delicate plants the winter protection they need, as well as providing you with the space to start preparing the blooms for next year's pots and borders.

But if you have got the time and the inclination then treat yourself to a free-standing greenhouse. But what sort of frame? Aluminium is light and less expensive, while a wooden one is more costly but will give you insulation on very cold and very hot days. You might also want to consider leaving one full side as glass to allow in more light in summer for tender vegetables and fruit.

But whatever you decide, go for one as big as possible, as there's no such thing as a greenhouse that's too big. (And remember to site it running east to west if possible.)

Aluminium greenhouses usually come in a pack for 'easy' self-assembly, but will need to be erected on firm ground or concrete slabs. A wooden greenhouse is trickier and will need footings (concrete underpinning) and a course of bricks, which needs to be dead square because the panes of glass have been cut to fit, and don't bend easily! At this stage it's worth setting a pipe or piece of hose through the footings too, so that the electrics can be threaded through later.

Without a little help a greenhouse is not 'frost free'. A lean-to has the added advantage of the warmth from a house wall, but an unheated greenhouse is only a degree or two warmer than outside. Basic protection for overwintering plants can be provided by bubble wrap, pinned or clipped on the inside of the glass.

Staging and shelving are also a must and can be bought as a kit or homemade. Then, (in order of importance!) come a radio, propagators, heating and a watering system. Heating will not only keep you warm but a minimum night-time temp of 4–5 °C will be sufficient to satisfy the needs of a wide range of plants.

18. An informal affair

If you have a large enough kitchen, then the freedom of a freestanding design is very hard to beat.

This is part of the appeal of such rooms – that everything in the space doesn't have to match perfectly. There might be modern items alongside more traditional pieces, and you might have pine mixed with oak or chrome mixed with wood.

You need a fairly large room to get away with a freestanding kitchen. All the elements will take up much more floor space than a fitted design. But if you do have such a luxury, then you can really enjoy putting together a room over a period of time. Put the basics in – your cooker, fridge, sink, etc. – but then rummage around for junk buys to complement your room and allow the scheme to grow over months or years.

There are certain things to bear in mind when putting together your floor plan for the room: foremost is that you need space around each item in the room. Try to visualise the different areas that you are going to need – the preparation area, the cooking space, the storage area and, if the room is large enough, the eating and seating area too.

In a kitchen where the walls will not be covered with cupboards, you need to consider what type of splashback you require on the walls. It's clearly vital around the cooking and food preparation areas, so what are your choices? Stainless steel will fit with a modern kitchen and you can buy ready-made panels to fit behind the cooker, while glass allows you to see through to the surface behind so would be perfect if there is a paint effect on your walls. Tiles are the norm and within everyone's budget, but if you have the cash splash out on granite for a stunning effect when combined with a work surface in the same material.

19. Turn on to bulbs

Bulbs and corms are just packed with energy. Treat 'em right and you can enjoy years of colour.

From hyacinths to tulips, crocuses to snowdrops, bulbs are one of the safest bets when it comes to guaranteed spring colour but there are a few general rules to follow.

It pays to buy your bulbs early as the condition in which they're stored is just as important as the soil you eventually plant them in. They need to have been kept cool and dry, not hot and bothered on a shop shelf.

You also need to avoid the temptation of buying a job lot. Of course they look good value but with bulbs the biggest really are the best, as they tend to be the ones that produce the best blooms on the strongest stems. The other bonus about buying them loose is that you can check each one, making sure it's not soft or diseased.

Bulbs need to be cold to get them going, which is why there's always such a rush of activity in the autumn, as gardeners are faced with a heap of the scaly brutes to intern.

Bulbs enjoy free draining soil so if you garden on clay add some grit or bulb fibre to the planting hole, and the more random your planting, the better the overall effect. Drop a handful of bulbs on the ground and plant them where they land.

Once in the ground, bulbs need little maintenance but will appreciate a handful of bonemeal after flowering to store up energy for next year.

Once they've done their bit, resist the urge to cut back the dying leaves too soon, as you'll weaken the bulb, and reduce its flowering potential for next year.

If you choose to leave your bulbs *in situ* all year it pays to dig them up and separate them every few years to prevent overcrowding. And if you've got any particularly expensive varieties in the ground mark their position so you don't inadvertently disturb them when they're dormant.

20. That hits the spot

Placing furniture can affect the mood of the room and how it is used. The lounge is a good room to use for this exercise.

If you want to create a formal look, keep pieces of furniture square on to each other, chair backs should be flat against walls and tables put at right angles to chairs. Keep coffee table books in carefully stacked piles of two or three diminishing in size from bottom to top. In contrast, chairs placed at an angle in the corners of rooms, sofas placed to create an L-shape or things displayed at random will seem much more relaxed.

Draw a floor plan of your room. Try and be accurate with the scaled-down measurements so that you have a realistic idea of how much the chimneybreast sticks out into the space or how much extra floor area there is in the bay window. Remember to put any 'permanent' fixtures like radiators onto the plan and also indicate which way the doors open into the room. Light switches and power points need to be noted so that you don't obstruct them with furniture. Take the plan away with you and sitting somewhere else list all of the furniture that is currently in the room.

Now think about how you use the room and assess whether you need every piece that is in there or whether there is something missing that would make the room work more efficiently. For example, think about whether the coffee table is actually in the wrong place for people to reach it with ease when sitting on the sofa. Or is a lamp positioned so far away from a reading chair that it can't possible function as a task light?

Here are some things to consider when you are planning other rooms...

■ Hallway: Does the table by the front door make it difficult to negotiate the space and would a wall-mounted narrow shelf be better?

■ Bedroom: Is all the storage that you have in there essential or could a dressy cupboard be positioned on the landing in a recess at the top of the stairs?

■ Dining room: Would you be better to get rid of two half-height cabinets and replace them with a taller unit that will house the contents of both but free up floor space?

21. Living with the enemy

Weeds are incredibly successful plants, usually natives that have had centuries to adapt to the environment in which they grow, making them extremely hardy, and able to reproduce quickly and easily.

Remember that some wildlife thrives on weeds. Without stinging nettles, for instance, peacock, small tortoiseshell and red admiral butterflies would have nowhere to lay their eggs. Isn't that reason alone to leave a few growing away unobtrusively at the back of the border?

There are two main types of weed, the annual and the perennial. Annuals like groundsel and cleavers can generally be cleared by decapitating them with a hoe. This is best done on a dry day, when you can leave them to wither away. When the soil's damp, just pull them out by hand, a very therapeutic way to get closer to your plants.

Perennials like stinging nettles, docks and dandelions, require a bit more effort and need digging out with a fork, root 'n' all. Pull up as much of the root as possible as they can grow back from the merest piece left in the ground.

Ground elder can quite happily smoother several square feet a year, while the horsetail does a lot of its work underground, entangling its black roots with those of other plants, making it even harder to get rid off. Thorough and repeated digging is the best approach, although it can have even the most dedicated organic gardener dreaming of weedkiller.

With its white trumpet flowers, there are certainly uglier plants than greater bindweed, which is actually part of the convolvulus family, cultivars of which we quite happily grow in the garden. The trouble is it doesn't know when to stop and will just keep on climbing unless kept in check. Organically, this means getting to grips with the fleshy, underground stems in early spring.

Perhaps the most invasive weed is Japanese knotweed, which has even been known to push up its shoots through thick concrete. Trying to defeat it is useless. You need to work round it, and just keep cutting it back.

Mulching is also a good way of keeping the likes of bindweed and couchgrass at bay. Remove what you can first of all and then spread a liberal layer of garden compost. This will starve the seeds of the light they need.

22. A piece of the past

Bring classic style to your home with traditional furniture and furnishings.

The year in which your home was built, the architectural details included in each room and the overall ambience of the place will lead you towards a particular look. Don't be too rigid in your interpretation though unless you want to live in a museum – it could leave you with a 'repressed' room. Stay in sympathy with your chosen style but feel free to allow one or two quirky elements to creep in to create a more relaxed environment.

You have really lucked out if your house already has particular features that reflect its age. An original fireplace or architectural mouldings like dado or picture rails, wood panelling, cornicing or even a tiled floor could all be the starting point for your design. Treat all of your original gems with respect. Too often people rip them out without due regard for how this will change the face of the place. But don't despair if you lack these kinds of details, they are easily introduced. Original and reproduction antique fires and mantelpieces can be sourced from manufacturers and reclamation yards. Wood mouldings are simple to fix in place by anyone with even a smidgen of DIY ability and are available in a mix of shapes and styles to suit.

Fabrics have an important role in the period home. Depending on the theme you'll want to look out for sumptuous silk, delicate lace, floral patterned chintzes, heavy damasks or richly coloured velvets. Consider how they were used in the past and you can introduce them today. You could pleat silk and use it as a wall covering for example, a lace panel may make a perfect table runner and a length of velvet might make an ideal throw.

The shape of furniture can also influence a mood. Introduce a heavy, imposing mahogany piece for a Victorian-style bedroom or a streamlined sofa in an art deco lounge.

From Shaker style to art nouveau and from the eighteenth century to the present day, certain colours are associated with certain styles. If you are looking for a guide you'll find period collections available wherever you shop for paint. It's important to get your walls the right shade because they provide the backdrop to the furniture and furnishings that will dress your room.

23. Getting fruity

Picking fruit from your own tree is one of the ultimate horticultural highs.

In the last thirty years, half of Britain's pear orchards and over sixty per cent of its apple orchards have been destroyed. So what better time to start planting some of the fabulously named traditional varieties of British fruit, from the Kentish Fillbasket apple to the Vicar of Winkfield pear?

First up, always buy trees from a reputable supplier, who specialises in fruit and can answer the following questions.

Is the tree on the right rootstock? All fruit trees are grafted onto roots that have been specially selected for the size and shape of tree they will ultimately support. They are identified by the letter M followed by a number. The rootstock determines the vigour, resistance to pests and disease, and the eventual formation of the tree. Only buy trees on recommended rootstocks, as these are also the only ones guaranteed virus free.

How does the tree pollinate? If the tree is a self-pollinator it will produce fruit all by itself. If not, it will need another tree, of a different variety, with which to 'mate'. Find out from a specialist book or nursery which varieties are compatible. It may be that one exists nearby in a neighbour's garden. If not, you'll need to do some matchmaking.

What growing conditions does the tree require? Take account of the area you live in, the space and shelter you can offer the tree, and the soil type.

Horticultural developments mean that you can now buy apples and pears that have been trained to specific shapes. Cordons grow at a 45° angle, while espaliers have a main vertical stem with horizontal tiers. Both are great space savers and can be grown against a wall or along a wire frame.

Step-over apples are espalier trees with the upward growth pruned out above the first set of horizontal branches, and provide excellent low 'walls' around the vegetable garden. Espaliers too can be used as decorative, productive screens.

24. Hot stuff

Combine functionality with style when heating your home.

Your fireplace should be the dramatic focal point of your room, so it needs to be in keeping with your chosen colour scheme and style.

Think of your various heat sources as pieces of furniture. You wouldn't just stick any old sofa in your lounge or any old cabinet in the kitchen – they need to match the mood and the same applies to radiators, fireplaces or stoves.

If you have inherited a fireplace with a dark slate surround and you want to use a white colour scheme in the room, then switch it for a design in limestone or one of the modern materials that fire manufacturers have developed that allow an amazing amount of detail to be moulded to the design.

The Swedish know how to do stoves. Their homes often feature grand ceramic designs, tiled or left plain, which can reach from floor to ceiling and make a magnificent feature in a room. Stoves can offer the ideal solution if you don't have a fireplace but want some kind of focal point to heat the room. They don't have to be huge or old fashioned and there are designs to run on any type of fuel.

There is no excuse for living with the classic ugly white radiators that you probably inherited with your home. In a modern setting change them for long spring-shaped designs that can run around the room just above skirting board height. Or choose one of the many contemporary shapes available: you can even buy a cactus-shaped radiator these days, or if you are looking for something to go in the children's room a design shaped like a big bear. Radiators can also be used as features in a room. Find a design that can also function as a room divider and you combine two elements, heating and design.

25. Blow raspberries

Whatever your age, juicy, sweet berries are a summertime delight but which types and varieties suit which garden? And can you really grow a blackberry without prickles?

The beauty of berries is that they provide a quick return after planting, but while strawberries, raspberries and blackberries share some common ground, such as a preference for moist, well-drained soil that's mildly acid, their growing habits and cultivation techniques are all significantly different.

Strawberries

For some, strawberries are the ultimate summer fruit. To get the best from strawbs, plant them in July or August to fruit the following summer. The plants prefer an open sunny spot with plenty of space between them, and need to be kept well watered, especially in spring when the fruits are swelling. To keep the berries off the ground, where they can fall prey to slugs or rot, surround the plants with straw (one of many theories behind the plant's name) or strawberry mats, making sure the ground is moist first. As a final deterrent, net them to protect from the birds.

Raspberries

This prickly customer is relatively easy to grow, crops best in full sun and can last up to 20 years. Before planting dig a trench, fill it with plenty of muck and mix in an all-round fertiliser. As the canes grow, cover them at the base with compost or grass cuttings to keep in the moisture, making sure the soil you're covering is already damp. But while they mustn't be allowed to dry out, water-logging can be just as harmful. Plant summer fruiting raspberries in autumn, feeding and mulching in spring.

Blackberries

Blackberries are one of the most abundant fruits in nature's larder and throughout September blackberrying is one of those few pastimes that seems to appeal to all ages. They enjoy the same rich, moist soils as the other berries but are a little less fussy. Plant in the autumn and immediately cut the stems down to just one bud. Each year, once fruiting has finished, cut down the stems that have fruited to allow new ones to develop. Make this easy by separating out the stems as they grow and training them against a fence.

26. Eating in

Relax at home with a dedicated dining space.

Of course there are many occasions when we want to go out and eat. But if you set up a dedicated dining space at home which has all the attributes of a good restaurant and none of the bad (leave the food aside at the moment), then you might find just as much pleasure in staying in and getting the friends to come to you.

If you need to eat in a corner of the kitchen or at one end of the lounge you will need to choose furniture that fits in the space. Look for adaptable tables that can expand to accommodate a group of people and that fold up when they aren't in use. Whatever style of dining chair you fancy, make sure that it's one that can stack.

You can indulge your desire for a very specific look if you have a separate dining room. Whatever the style of the rest of your home, should you wish for ruby red walls, rich velvet-covered seats, a dramatic chandelier and floor-standing candelabras, then here's the space where you can create that look. The room described above will call for gold or silver chargers set beneath the finest china with exquisite glasses for red wine, white wine and water, teamed with fine cutlery and the finest starched table linen. Now if you usually eat from plain white plates, eat with plastic-handled knives and fork and use a handy chunky tumbler for a glass of red wine, these items will not translate into your designer dining room. My point is that you will need to invest in a complete set of glasses, platters, cutlery and serving spoons, mats and all the associated tableware to make such an extravagant scheme work. Do you have the budget to do that or should you work to design a room which will work with items that you already own?

You can treat the preparation of your dining room as putting together a puzzle. The design of the room is the main part of the image and you need all the other pieces in place for it to look complete. Whether you are having a formal dinner to impress the guests or a casual meal for good friends, the same principles apply.

27. To prune or not...?

Take a moment or two to learn the whys, whens and hows of basic pruning, and who knows, you might find it so much fun you take up topiary!

Pruning inspires plants; it's a chemical thing that makes them grow back in a different way. It may be a bit of an oxymoron but cutting plants back hard will stimulate rapid growth.

The basic pruning set should include a good pair of secateurs (for cutting stems and twigs up to 1cm thick), a pruning saw (for smaller branches), loppers for any hard to reach tough stuff, and garden shears for trimming soft growth. Try tackling everything with the same pair of blunt kitchen scissors and you'll be rewarded with mashed stems and a nice line in blisters.

Most plants need an annual prune to keep them healthy and productive. Just removing dead wood and any stems that are rubbing against each other (so letting in disease) can give the most dishevelled shrub a new lease of life. And a cut in the right place, at the right time, can encourage side shoots, fruiting spurs and flowers. Many roses, soft fruits and fruiting trees need pruning in the dormant season – that time when they're asleep, from autumn through to early spring. Trained fruit trees will need summer pruning as well to keep them in shape.

Shrubs however fall into two main groups and while it's not difficult, if you get it wrong, you'll have to wait another year to see any flowers. If the shrub flowers in spring, on branches grown in the previous year – forsythia is a typical example – prune it after flowering. If you mistakenly cut it hard back before flowering, you'll be taking out the stems that are covered in buds. The second group are shrubs that flower later in the year, on the current year's growth, such as buddleia. Pruning these in early spring will encourage them to produce fresh growth that will flower later that summer.

There is a third group – slow growing shrubs that keep the same basic shape, e.g magnolia, azaleas, witch hazel and the hardy hibiscus. Leave these alone except for the pruning out of dead or damaged wood.

28. A tough decision

Choose stone floors for their looks and durability.

There is something about stone that says timeless luxury. Is it because we know that these materials have formed over millions of years and so deserve to be treated with the respect and deference that their age commands? Or is just that we are familiar with seeing them used in grand houses and historic buildings which make them an object of desire?

Marble is to floors what diamonds are to jewellery: an expensive choice but one that rewards you with its sheer beauty and dramatic impact on the eye. In sheet form it is always going to break the bank (sort of like a four-carat emerald-cut stone), but there is the less pricey alternative of tiles, although these are more likely to be a backing material with a veneer of marble laid on top. Marble is one of those materials that makes a real statement. It needs to be used in big spaces and grand locations. That's why you find it used in luxury hotel foyers.

Granite is in the luxury goods department too. The choice of colours, from pink-hued and speckled white to blue-grey and black, means it can fit in with most colour schemes. Just be careful if you choose a polished finish as this will make it slippery. Slate has a much more rustic appeal, and if you want an immaculately smooth finish to your floors look elsewhere. It can be slightly rough with worn edges, but its waterproof qualities make it a good choice in the bathroom, for example.

If you are looking for a lighter option consider sandstone and limestone. In creamy whites, buttery yellows and pale grey, these would be suited to areas where you need a floor in keeping with a light colour scheme. (Some of these are named after the area in which they are quarried just to confuse you: Cotswold stone, for example is a limestone.) Now if these floors are laid properly, sealed and maintained they will look great. However, because they are porous they will easily stain so make sure that you get them treated. For that same reason you must also be careful about the type of cleaning solution that you use. A black mark in the middle of a large expanse of light stone will ruin the luxury look, and you can't just scrub it off with bleach.

29. Hedging your bets

Hedges are a long-term project but there's a lot to be gained from planting a wall of box or yew.

So why do you want a hedge? Is it purely a decorative feature, or are you looking to create a screen to ensure some privacy and cut out noise? Perhaps you want to establish a boundary, need a windbreak, or simply want to attract wildlife? A mixed, informal hedge covers most options. Hazel, hawthorn, beech, and hornbeam are some of the most common. In the right place, a conifer hedge does still have a lot going for it – all you need to do is monitor it closely and make sure it's kept at a manageable height.

It's essential to plant up a new hedge in the late autumn, as the plants will need time to find their feet before the first growing period the following spring. Apart from the usual organic matter, some bonemeal will help them on their way. These first six months are the most critical period so water at the first sign of a dry spell, and resist the urge to clip them, however unkempt their appearance.

There are two essentials you need to consider first. Proportion – in a small garden, the last thing you want is a hedge soaring 20 ft up in the air, blocking out all your light, with thirsty roots turning the ground beneath it into a dust bowl. If time is on your side try yew, which is a relatively slow grower. Given acid to neutral free-draining soil it will add 30cm a year but it does give the richest of greens and is one of the few evergreens that allows you to prune back into old wood. In a hurry? Cypress is a speed merchant growing at 1m a year! Other shrubs not normally associated with hedges, but which perform perfectly well, are the ornamental plum or the purple berberis. The thick evergreen escallonia macrantha will help maintain your privacy.

You can add more life and colour to your hedge by encouraging other plants to grow through it. Honeysuckle's the leading contender along with varieties of rose and clematis, while it's not uncommon for a blackberry bush to self seed and put in a welcome appearance.

30. Perchance to dream

When considering how you want your bedroom to look start with the style, which will dictate colour choices, fabric types and furniture design, and bear in mind that there are endless variations on these themes.

Yellows and greens or rosy pinks can form the basis for the scheme that gives a rustic feel. Keep a light touch when decorating. Opt for wallpaper with a delicate print, and if you can't face papering every wall, then just use it in alcoves or on the wall facing the door. Choose carpet for the floor and reflect that cosy mood with wool blankets on the bed or a patchwork quilt that matches your colour scheme. Indulge yourself with a curvy wrought iron bedstead and plump for painted or pine wooden furniture for storage. Lamps with pleated fabric shades would be apposite for the bedside table, as would a blanket box positioned at the end of the bed.

Work with a colour scheme including white, shades of grey, cream and brown for an oriental feel. The mood is minimalist so hide or disguise clutter in the room. Opt for a laminate or real wood floor that you can dress up with rugs for extra comfort. Select natural linens to deck out the bed, calico or cotton pillowslips, for example, and put wooden Venetian blinds or shutters at the window. A low-level wooden bed would suit this style, and fitted wardrobes would contribute to the clean lines of the space.

For a classic style consider a muted yellow or duck egg blue as the starting point for your scheme. It may be appropriate to pick a patterned carpet so you will need to choose your bed linen to co-ordinate accordingly. Curtains are a must. If you want to add a dressy pelmet at the window then echo this look with a canopied bed and be lavish in your use of fabric. Feel free to introduce a gilded mirror or arrange classic prints across one wall. It suits the mood to display a collection of perfume bottles or perhaps have an antique set of brushes and hand held mirror on display. A slipper chair, fabric-covered ottoman or chaise longue will add the finishing touch. Given that we spend up to a third of our lives in the bedroom, it is worth getting a style that works morning and night, summer and winter to fulfil every requirement.

31. On the waterfront

It's very easy to allow a pond to dominate a garden. But if your aim is to attract frogs, newts and dragonflies, then the smallest wet area will do.

Here are a few things to consider:

- Formal or informal? Formal requires a lot more work, can look out of place in an otherwise informal garden and isn't much loved by wildlife.
- If the idea of running water appeals, then work this out carefully before starting on any construction.
- Ideally site your pond in partial shade, away from deciduous trees, whose leaves will clog it up in autumn.

When marking out the pond with pegs, take the time to make sure they're level. And although plants will help upset any symmetry, remember this is an informal pond, so avoid perfect squares and circles. The size and depth is up to you, although 1m in the middle should be the max – it hardly needs saying that young children can drown in the shallowest of ponds. Around the edge you need a shallow ledge to enable creatures to crawl out, with flat bottomed terraces and shelves on which to lodge baskets.

Remove any heavy or sharp stones, and then line generously with soft sand before laying a single piece of butyl liner over the whole area, making sure it extends beyond the pond's edge. Cover the bottom with about 10cm of earth, again devoid of sharp stones, for direct planting or as a 'bed' for your baskets to sit on. You can now fill with water – rain or tap – and then trim the excess liner.

Shading the surface of your pond from direct sunlight with surface plants or overhanging trees will help the water stay clear and algae free. But net the pond in autumn to prevent dead leaves falling in and contaminating the water. Installing a small pump will help keep the water aerated and grace you pond with either a fountain or trickle feature. Electrics are required here and must be handled by a professional. Clean and check the pump once a year.

Submerge a stocking packed with barley straw to combat blanket weed – believe me you'll experience this sooner or later. It may be an old wives tale but usually has some impact. Pull the green cobweb-like weed out whenever you can too, and leave it on the side for a day so any small water creatures can crawl back into the pond.

32. Blind ambition

A lovely window treatment doesn't have to rely on swathes of fabric.

The beauty of blinds is that they sit neatly in their designated space. And if you think they are too plain, then think again. A patterned fabric made into a blind can have just as much impact as a dressy curtain.

Your windows may be at the very edge of your room but they can take up a large proportion of the wall space and need the same consideration that you give to your paint colour or choice of wallpaper. If your walls are painted in a single colour, you can use your choice of blind to introduce an interesting contrast to the space. If you have chosen to hang a patterned paper, then a plain blind may be just what you need.

Roller blinds bring simplicity to a window – just a flat piece of fabric that neatly rolls away. Dress up a plain roller with a contrasting panel oe stencilling at the bottom. If you are thinking about a treatment for your bedroom and need to preserve your privacy, choose a bottom-up design. With a box fitted to the window sill (preferably), or outside the bottom of the frame (this can look bulky), you raise them up rather than drop them down. This means the bottom half the window can remain covered while the top is clear to allow light into the room.

One of the greatest new innovations for rollers is the huge variety of pulls from which you can now choose; wooden blocks, jute balls, leather laces and ceramic beads can all be added to the bottom of your blind if you feel the need to dress it up a bit.

Roman blinds have clean lines: the pleats sit neatly when they are open and the fabric lies flat when they are closed. Reefed blinds make a more quirky statement but can end up being a pain to operate and keep looking neat. These are pulled up and down by cords, which run through eyelets at the top of the blind and loop down and around the fabric. This means you can pull them up very tight, but you often have to fiddle with the fabric to allow it to roll up neatly.

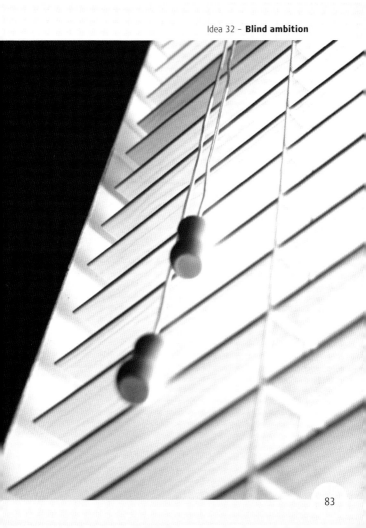

33. Winter wonderland

A garden with winter interest makes work for idle hands and gives you the chance to enjoy those plants that actually look their best on a cold and frosty morning.

If you plant evergreens for interest, and train and clip trees to give shape, your garden need never loose its sense of form. Even the hard landscaping provided by paths, steps, paving and walls helps to keep the garden together, while a well-chosen trellis, support or arch can provide a new, seasonal focal point.

If you're not an over tidy gardener, then leave standing border plants with unusual seed-heads – such as phlomis, sedum, eryngiums – well alone and enjoy their frosted shapes. Similarly, soft brown grasses can look warm and mellow in the winter light. If you do go for this approach, everything will need cutting back in February, before the new growth appears.

The coloured stems of the dogwood range from bright green and yellow through to scarlet, wine red and almost black. They're a must for winter colour, while the vivid, violet berries of Callicarpa bodinieri look positively tropical, and just about last into December.

It's staggering how many small flowers can survive the winter weather. Appearing in early January, the delicate snowdrops reliably force their heads through the cold, hard ground and go well with aconites and hellebores. For the best chance of getting snowdrops to take, and then colonise, buy them after they've finished flowering, when they're still 'green', and plant them where they won't dry out in summer.

A topping of snow along the box hedges reinforces their shape, while a sprinkle around the low-growing black grass (Ophiopogon planiscapus 'Nigrescens') shows off its striking foliage. But if there's a heavy covering keep an eye on upright growing conifers, and shake off the snow before it bends or snaps the branches. A delicate covering of frost is also to be enjoyed, as long as you've taken all the right precautions to protect your tender plants and pots. Those that need their centres guarding against the cold, such as the tree fern and cordyline, should be wrapped up with straw, surrounded by chicken wire. Pots should be taken into a frost free, sheltered place, or covered in bubble wrap or hessian, and raised off the ground.

34. What's cooking?

Take the fitted approach to streamline your kitchen. The beauty of investing in a fitted kitchen is that it can be tailor-made to suit all the quirky corners or awkward shapes that exist in most homes.

It's also a way of maximising space and can provide some brilliant storage solutions, designed to make your life that much easier. With the luxury of starting from scratch you can make sure that the light is right, that the power points are in the correct places for all your gadgets, and that your day-to-day use of the space is a joy.

The triangle principle
This is an age-old device that kitchen planners have been promoting for years when they start to lay out the room. It goes like something like this: the cooking area, preparation area and storage should each be at the point of a triangle so that you can move efficiently between the three work areas. It has its limits because everybody cooks in a different way. While the sink may be one of your three important areas if you don't own a dishwasher, if you do it means your priorities will be different. And with microwaves replacing

ovens for a lot of people, that lovely high-tec fan/gas/electric combi-cooker may only be used at the weekends. You want a layout that suits you for more than two days a week.

If the number of people hanging around the Ikea kitchen department on a Saturday morning is any indication, you'd think putting together a kitchen required a degree in design. It doesn't, but the sheer volume of options for cupboard doors, work surfaces, appliances, etc., can be intimidating. It does help when you are planning a kitchen, probably more than any other room in the house, if you can make a decision. If you are the kind of person who takes half an hour to choose which toppings you want on your pizza, give yourself a year to put your room together.

35. Scentsational

Sit back in a deck chair surrounded by the heady fragrance of a well-positioned honeysuckle, or the calming scent of lavender, and suddenly all the hard work seems worthwhile.

Scent is evocative: smell hyacinths and you think of spring; sweet peas mingled with the aroma of freshly cut grass and summer holidays come flooding back; while bonfires and fallen leaves mean that autumn's approaching. Fortunately, most types of plants come in scented forms from shrubs to climbers, perennials to annuals. But it's not just a question of choosing the right ones, you also need to place them where they will be truly appreciated.

Arches, pergolas, even the porch are all crying out to be smothered in aromatic blooms. Honeysuckle is a traditional choice. The deciduous type is slightly less rampant than the evergreen version but both have delicious scent. The romantics, of course, will choose roses, particularly climbers like the pink Mme Grégoire Staechelin, New Dawn or Zephrin Drouhun. You can prolong their interest too by combining them with a contrasting coloured clematis – sadly not fragrant, while Rosa englanteria will cover a fence with aromatic foliage and fill the air with the smell of fresh apples.

Freesias are less commonly grown but F. 'Yellow River' and F. alba in particular, have good perfume. They grow from half-hardy corms, flowering late winter to early spring, if given a sheltered site. Dig up after flowering and dry them off ready to replant in the autumn.

Another unusual plant worth growing for its scent, shape and pale yellow flowers is the tree lupin (Lupinus arboreus). Don't panic, it's only a 1.5m shrub and will not get out of bounds as sadly, it is short-lived. Also include for scent, if your garden is not too cold, the deep purple-pink Daphne meseerum or the paler D. odora. Remember too the sunnier the position the greater the scent.

A wisteria wrapped round a garden shed, or hovering over the compost heap, smacks of bad planning. Its subtle clove-like scent will be wasted. Scented plants need to be close at hand – you need to be able to smell them as you take in the early spring sunshine. So, either move a seat near to them, or if that's not practical, plant up the area around a fixed seat with those fragrant plants that will wow your senses, like pots of lilies – the most fragrant are Lilium candidum (Madonna Lily) or L. regale.

36. Light up your life

There's a good, a bad and a downright ugly way of lighting any space.

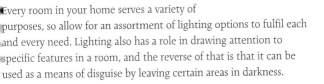

Every room in your home serves a variety of purposes, so allow for an assortment of lighting options to fulfil each and every need. Lighting also has a role in drawing attention to specific features in a room, and the reverse of that is that it can be used as a means of disguise by leaving certain areas in darkness.

You can reduce lighting to three basic types, and to create a successful scheme you need to layer all three: ambient, task and accent lighting. Ambient light is designed to offer an all-over well-lit room. This is the starting point to any scheme and the most basic type of lighting. Task lighting, as the name suggests, works to illuminate specific tasks. These might be working at your computer, applying your make-up or cooking. Its purpose is to provide enough light for the activity concerned – enough to prevent eyestrain. Accent lighting is the type that can often be neglected but brings out the best in a room. It will highlight the best features such as works of art, pieces of furniture or a particular area – a dining table in a kitchen/diner is a classic example.

Here are ideas for each room:

Stairs: Position a recessed spot light or low-level wall washer beside every second or third step, making sure you have an on/off switch at the bottom and top.

Lounge: Why not avoid an overhead light altogether and have an electrician put two or three lamps on a circuit that is operated by a single switch? If you have shelving in alcoves either side of a chimneybreast, then use down-lighters to highlight the items that are displayed.

Kitchen: Include lights that run underneath wall-mounted cabinets as well as your overhead strip or spots. Have the different lights on separate circuits so you can use as much or as little light as you need. This will also mean you can transform a practical and functional working area into somewhere appropriately lit for an intimate dinner party.

Bedroom: You must have lights at either side of the bed.

Bathroom: Make sure that you can see to cleanse your face. An illuminated mirror is a must.

37. Alright mate

Companion planting is one of those ideas that's so simple and so obvious it should be made compulsory in every garden. It's the organic way of keeping pests at bay, and while it has its critics, organic gardeners know it works.

There are several different ways in which plants help each other. Many destructive insects locate their food by smell, so by interplanting possible targets with other plants that have a strong scent, you can confuse the enemy. A second way is that some plants, through scent, colour and pollen, attract predatory insects into the garden. These predators will then seek and destroy the harmful insects which were about to have a good chew on your plants. And a third group virtually sacrifice themselves for the cause, luring the bad bugs away from the more valuable crops, to have a go at them instead.

However you look at it, companion planting is not good news for the humble aphid. Garlic underneath roses is one way to keep greenfly at bay, but if any do get through, a sprig or two of dill nearby will attract wasps and hoverflies to hoover up the stragglers.

Aphids also turn their proboscis up at chervil, which is good interplanted with lettuce, and they don't much care for coriander either. Yarrow (Achillea millefolium) is a fine flowering plant for the veg patch and another one that draws in the predators, including ladybirds, who love nothing better than an aphid picnic.

One of the best vegetable combos is carrots and leeks, because while the latter repels carrot fly, the former gives off a smell offensive to the onion fly and leek moth (yes, apparently there is such a thing). Another good double act sees tomatoes, with a bit of basil, deterring the asparagus beetles, while chemicals in the asparagus itself help prevent a harmful nematode attacking the roots of the tomato plant. Tomatoes are also one of the main beneficiaries of being mixed up with French marigolds.

There are plenty of possible combinations and a few cases where the chemicals in one plant can actually inhibit the growth of another. So it pays to keep a gardening diary to note down the combinations that work, and those that don't.

38. Bathe in style

A well-designed bathroom is a versatile space.

The starting point for planning a new bathroom can often be a list of the faults of the existing one. If you are going to revamp a bathroom, you need to decide whether you want to keep the existing layout and replace fixtures where they are, or move things in, out and around to get better use of what is, more often than not, a spatially challenged room.

Bidets are incredibly useful. Here are some uses (other than the purpose it was designed for) to explain why, if you have the space, you should fit the fourth piece into your suite of bath, basin and WC.

- There's always somewhere to leave the hand-laundry soaking.
- It is the perfect place for washing feet pre-pedicure.
- If you can't use the loo to be sick you have another receptacle.

With both bidets and toilets always opt for wall-hung designs, for one simple reason: cleaning around pedestals is a pain, and they are a place where dirt tends to gather. The joy of being able to mop across a floor unhindered by the usual obstructions has to be experienced to be really understood.

Cast-iron baths weigh a ton. If you are looking to recreate the look of a period bathroom, check that your floor will take the weight. Also remember that with a freestanding bath the amount of water that splashes over the edge will increase considerably (more sides for the bath water to slop over) so you do need flooring that will withstand regular soakings. While the idea of picking up an old fashioned piece from reclamation yards may have a romantic appeal, don't bother. Brand new is easily affordable and reproduction designs are so good that I would buy new every time.

If you live with a partner or have kids, fit in a double sink wherever possible. There is great pleasure in having your own sink.

Design your bathroom to fit your family and you'll reap the rewards for years to come.

39. Wildlife friendly

A garden without wildlife is a pretty sorry sight. No bird song, no pollinating insects, no frogs or toads lurking behind the garden shed. No fun.

There are four basics you need to provide to attract wildlife – food, water, shelter and somewhere to breed.

Try and find room in the garden for plants that wildlife enjoy, such as the seed-heavy teasels, sunflowers and thistles, or the berry-laden cotoneasters and hollies. They look great and birds will love them. Grow plants that are rich in pollen and nectar too, such as Verbena bonariensis, buddleia, sedums, eupatorium and nepeta. As well as pollinators, these will also attract predatory insects into the garden such as ladybirds and lacewings which will lay their eggs on the plants. In due course these will hatch into larvae, which are the aphid eating machines of the insect world.

The simplest of water features can make a difference, even an old washing bowl sunk into the ground in a quiet corner of the garden, part-filled with stones, will attract frogs and toads. And you can give nature a helping hand by asking friends with ponds both for a jar of bug rich pond water, and any spare frog spawn they've got lying about. Bird baths are also important, both as a source of fresh drinking water and as somewhere to bathe.

Try and find an area of the garden you can let grow wild, where plants like stinging nettles can flourish. This 'weed' plays an important part in the lifecycle of over 100 different species of insect, including several butterflies. In winter dead and decaying plants add an air of mystery to any border, as well as providing refuge for overwintering insects.

The likes of beech, blackthorn, hazel, hornbeam and hawthorn are excellent trees when it comes to offering wildlife shelter. And log piles are hotels with 24 hour room service to many bugs, hedgehogs and grass snakes. The insects and fungi that gradually eat the wood will, in turn, feed other creatures in the garden.

Garden birds, particularly nesting ones, devour caterpillars, leatherjackets and chafer grubs as well as slugs and snails. So a few well-sited nesting boxes, out of the reach of your pet moggy, will work wonders.

40. Keep it tidy

If you are going to declutter you need to approach it with dedication and verve and, most importantly, with a lack of sentimentality.

Pick a room – any room – and sit in the middle. What you are about to do is remove roughly one-quarter of the contents in that space. That's your target. (And that's just for starters. You should go back a week later and repeat the process.)

Kitchen: Chuck out unused spices, old tins, battered bakeware, chipped crockery, fraying table linen, knackered saucepans and unused gadgets (bread makers and juicers being chief culprits).
Lounge: Get rid of books, China ornaments that were dodgy holiday mementoes or suspect gifts, dried flower arrangements, worn out cushions and old CDs.
Bedroom: Give many, *many* items of clothing to the charity shop. If you keep your bed linen in there, how many sets do you realistically need? If you've mislaid one of a matching pair of pillowcases chuck the odd one out – if you take it to the kitchen to cut up and use as cleaning cloths you are only adding to the clutter down there, so chuck it.

Bathroom: Dispose of old make-up, old medicines, half-used body lotions and potions and towels that were stained by your last hair-dyeing experiment.

Start in the corner furthest away from the door. If there's a rug on the floor or a cushion that needs to go, take it out of the room and put it in a pile outside the door. If there's a cupboard in the corner, open the door and, starting from the top, take out everything that's on the shelf. For each item ask yourself when was the last time that you looked at it, read it, used it or even thought about it. If you can't remember any of the above then take it out of the room and add it to the pile. If the cupboard is not sectioned off, bring in some new storage systems: box files for papers, garments bags for clothes, etc. Take everything that you've removed and recycle it in the appropriate way.

Approach decluttering with the determination of a pitbull and you'll reap the rewards in terms of tidiness, cleanliness and lots of lovely extra space.

41. The can-can

All plants need water to survive, but how can we maximise its effect in the garden, while minimising waste?

Don't just 'splash it all over'. A long and thorough soak is much better than a gentle sprinkle – once a week rather than once a day. Only water when your plants need it and in summer never water during the day as it will have no lasting benefit and most of the water will simply evaporate. Best wait until the evening, so the water can do its bit overnight.

Try and get the water straight to the plant's roots. A garden sprinkler pointing up in the air will refresh the leaves but unless left on for hours, its spray will never reach the soil. Use a hosepipe on low pressure instead and aim it on the roots. Count to a hundred (two hundred if you can bear it) for each shrub or climbing plant, especially those having to compete for moisture, say under a tree or against a wall. Mature shrubs and trees should cope with dry conditions in most summers.

Making your soil as spongy as possible will help retain the moisture, and you can do this by adding well-rotted compost in autumn or spring each year. The final rule is to keep the soil cool. Covering it entirely with plants will help retain moisture, and minimise evaporation.

But for the butts a lot of water would be lost down the drain. There's a sense of satisfaction in getting something for free and collecting rainwater comes under this category. It's also coming straight from the heavens, so is free from contamination. Place two or three together with connecting pipes and the bulk of your watering needs will be met. Use green plastic butts where they're out of sight and old cider or sherry barrels for show.

42. Tread softly

Or more mundanely, where and why to use carpet.

Familiarise yourself with the jargon of carpets before you buy. The construction, pile, fibre content and texture are all points to consider. Clearly your biggest influence will probably be the colour but these other things need to be factored in. You want a carpet that will last so check a couple of things to give you an idea of how hardwearing it will be. Look at the back of woven carpets and make sure that the tufts are packed closely together. Kneel down or press the pile with the heel of your hand and make sure that it springs back quickly. Good quality woven carpets are sure to last. If you choose a tufted design, go for the most expensive you can afford.

If you are carpeting the whole house and need to cut costs, go for less expensive carpets in the bedroom and spend more money on areas that get constant use such as the hall, lounge and stairs.

With so many colour choices and such a wide range of textures, carpet is a valuable decorating tool when putting together your scheme. Because of the large amount of space that it covers, plain carpets in light colours will help to make a room seem much bigger. Using the same carpet through two or three small rooms will also create the illusion of a bigger home. Patterned designs have their place if you have kids or pets, helping to disguise wear and tear. If you have opted for plain walls and furnishings in a room, they also function as a tool for bringing in a mix of colours to the area.

Budget for good quality underlay: it prolongs the life of a carpet. It levels out any imperfections in the sub-floor, and is an effective way of preventing heat loss – on average 15% of heat loss from a home is through the floor. The thickest underlay is not necessarily the best, however. For a high quality option look for one that has been made by a carpet manufacturer from the yarn that is left over from the carpet-making process.

You want to walk over your floors in comfort for years to come so take the time to carefully consider the carpets.

43. Container gardening

Plants will grow in just about anything from ceramic vases to old watering cans, wooden planters to your own 'mock' rock troughs.

Terracotta pots are the pot of choice for most people. They look natural, age beautifully and are heavy enough to stand up to blustery conditions. But they're also very porous and unless you line them with something like a bin bag, with a few drainage holes added, this will soak up water before the plants get a look in. And stopping this water leaching into the terracotta also means they're less likely to crack when it freezes (and that goes for the so-called frost proof pots as well.)

The first thing to check with any container is that it has drainage holes at the bottom – if it doesn't, get the drill out. Next add some crocks, stones or old bits of polystyrene from broken up seed trays, to stop those vital drainage holes clogging up. An old cloth over the crocks will filter the water and stop your compost washing away.

Now for the compost itself. Tempting as it may be, avoid using garden soil as you don't know what pests and disease could be lurking in it. Better to use a loam based compost such as John Innes No2, or a general potting or multipurpose compost – peat-free of course. However, despite its impeccable green credentials, the downside of peat-free alternatives is that they dry out quicker than peat, so add a bit of leaf mould or garden compost, and some water retentive crystals too. For acid lovers like rhododendrons, you'll need to use lime-free ericaceous compost.

Plants in containers need regular attention and regular watering – rain isn't enough to keep them going (even in the winter you need to keep an eye on the dryness of the compost). Pellets of slow release fertiliser pressed into the soil are a good idea too, although the plants will also appreciate a fortnightly dose of tomato feed in summer.

Deadheading, replacing plants that are past their prime, and checking pots for any pests such as slugs or weevils that have had the audacity to climb in should all become part of you maintenance routine.

44. Work that room

You want a work area at home to be able to operate independently from the rest of the house.

If you aren't lucky enough to have a dedicated room you will need to create a space in another place and the dining room is a perfect spot for doubling up. There is already a table and chairs (although you should invest in a dedicated work chair – you are going to be sitting for several hours a day and don't want to end up with backache). You probably already have plenty of lamps and good dedicated lighting in the dining room and adding another piece of storage that won't look out of place shouldn't be too tricky if you pick a unit that matches your existing colour scheme.

If you need to adapt a corner of the lounge, try and make sure that you position your desk on the same side of the room as the door and preferably behind where it opens into the space. That way, if you don't tidy up at the end of everyday, a cluttered desk isn't the first thing that people see when they walk into the room.

Working from home raises a few specific issues.

Good communication is a must. Have a dedicated phone, fax and internet line for your work.

Organisation is essential. Make sure that you have enough storage. There is nothing more off-putting when you start the working day than piles of papers on the floor and a desk littered with literature.

Layout is key. Set up the space so that information you need instant access to is positioned near to the desk. Occasional reference material can go in a cupboard on the other side of the room.

Safety is an issue. Keep an eye on the number of plugs going into sockets and extension leads and keep cabling organised so that it doesn't get into a spaghetti-like state.

Lighting must be right. Get dedicated task lighting. Do position a lamp on your desk but don't allow it to reflect on the screen.

Avoid distractions: Position your office away from the busy or family areas of the home.

Make it a dedicated space. Try and keep the office area clear of anything that isn't related to your work.

If you try to implement as many of the above as possible, you should find working from home works for you.

45. The herb garden

**he beauty of herbs is that they'll go
nywhere – the corner of a mixed bed, a
ontainer or hanging basket, or just
lotted around the vegetable patch.**

Many herbs naturally grow on the sun-baked, well-drained soils of
Mediterranean countries, so choose a bright spot – near to the
kitchen door if you can. Most herbs prefer light, fertile soil and if
you garden on chalk you're laughing. Mint and parsley like moister
conditions. They do well in containers too – arrange those that
enjoy the same type of conditions together.

Here are others to consider.

Basil – annual herb much used in Italian and French cooking,
and with tomatoes. It likes full sun but loses its flavour when
frozen.

Thyme – a dwarf evergreen that you can harvest all-year round.
It needs good drainage and will grow happily in cracks between
paving slabs. There are green and gold forms.

Rosemary – at its best in full sun, it will grow into a small shrub
and makes a good, low-growing hedge around the front of a bed
of herbs.

- Tarragon – not fully hardy so make sure you give it some winter protection from frost. For taste, grow the French variety.
- Parsley – actually classed as a hardy biennial but for the best flavour, treat it as an annual. Low growing with curly or broad leaved varieties. Start if off in early spring under a cloche.
- Chives –throw up their mauve balls of colour in early summer and are great for the front of a bed or along a path. Dead head if you don't want it to self seed.
- Marjoram (or oregano) – beloved of pizza makers. A hardy perennial that has small mauve flowers in summer. Its bright golden green leaves and clump forming habit make it a good ground cover plant for the front of the shrub bed. Trim back in autumn and divide every three years.
- Dill – similar to fennel with feathery blue-green leaves on tall stems. Use fresh or dried.
- Coriander – you can eat the leaves and the ripe seeds of this low growing annual.

Of the more unusual herbs, horseradish is good value because not only do you get to use its hot, fiery root for sauce, but the young leaves can be used in a salad. A pot may be ideal though as once planted you will never get rid of the root.

46. Curtain call

There is a plethora of different looks for your curtains but you should always be generous with the fabric that you use.

Whatever the style of the room, the curtains should comfortably cover the window; if the fabric has to be pulled quite flat to meet in the middle they will always look cheap, cheap, cheap. Allow a minimum of twice the width of the window and a maximum of three when you buy it.

Those clever designs that seem effortlessly to pool on the floor can look amazing. This look works better with light fabric that flows and drapes easily; anything too heavy will bulk up on the floor into a heavy pile rather than sink down into a light pool.

Never buy fabric for curtains based on a tiny swatch. You will have no idea about how a print will look when it is made up into curtains if you have only seen a small square of the design. It would be a bit like buying a still-life when the artist has only sketched a single apple: how are you going to know what the overall finished piece will look like? The best way to get an idea when you are buying fabric for this job is to grab the roll off the shelf in the shop and pull out a metre or two so that you can see the complete repeat of a design.

Depending on the place that you are decorating, look to lovely shears, muslins and voiles for rooms where you want the light to flood in. They have a luxurious air when allowed to drape in generous swathes. One trick to add a more formal touch is to hang them behind a pelmet which is covered in a contrasting fabric. Choose damasks, heavy linen and textured silk when you want to make more of a statement with the drapes when they are closed. There is no doubt that you will have already made a decision about your colour scheme when you come to choose the fabric but think about the different effects that patterns can achieve. If you want to create the illusion of extra height, then opt for a design with a vertical stripe. If you want to add width, then pick a material with a horizontal design.

47. Trees for all

Choosing the right tree for your garden is possibly the most important horticultural decision you can make. So it pays to pick the right one.

For early blossom consider a flowering cherry, crab apple or the delicate pink blossom of the ornamental plum, one of the first to appear, and with the flowers closely followed by deep purple leaves. A rose-pink flowered version of the wild hawthorn, Crataegus laevigata 'Paul Scarlet', is also well worth considering for a small garden.

In spring, magnolia is hard to beat, although if you garden on chalk your only choice is the multi-stemmed Magnolia Stellata. It's hardy but in cold areas be prepared to cover it with fleece at night to protect the starry white flowers from frost. Two other possibilities with spring colour are the lilac, in its white, mauve and purple forms, and laburnum, which although poisonous is still a striking, slow-growing tree with graceful, yellow hanging flowers.

In summer a tree can be enjoyed close-up, so it needs to either complement surrounding plants or be a stunner in its own right, such as the variegated acer with its single straight stem and fabulous green, edged-white maple leaves. The false acacia has acid green foliage and looks good in a sheltered, sunny spot, and the honey locust has unusual, finely divided green and yellow leaves.

Autumn colour is a real boost as summer disappears. And the secret of those rusty reds and cheery yellows is all in the soil; the more acidic it is, the better the autumn colour. Maples are renowned for their autumnal colour but many grow into monsters so choose carefully. The Japanese maples are relatively small and grow well if sheltered from the wind. For a tough, uncomplicated little tree, with vibrant autumn colour choose the staghorn Sumach or the crab apple (Malus 'Golden Hornet') that has both golden fruit and yellow leaves in autumn.

Trees in winter are a dramatic feature of the sky line but there's interest close up too. Acer capillipes is not called the snake bark acer for nothing! The spindle tree (the deciduous Euonymous), on acid soil, turns flame red in autumn and its red berries, shaped like a cardinal's hat, are a favourite with robins in winter.

48. First impressions

Seen first and frequently passed through, your hallway deserves more attention than you may think.

Make it welcoming: A chair or reclaimed church pew that is tucked against the wall allows people to rest for a minute after they walk through the door.

Keep it useful: Coat hooks, umbrella stands, a mat to wipe feet on and a table to dump the post on make it a functional space

Light it right: Make sure that you have switches at the bottom and top of the staircase. If it's very dark, consider replacing a solid wood front door with a design that has glass panels.

Secure the door: Add as many devices as you want: bolts, chains and a spy hole are all advisable.

Choose a colour scheme that won't clash with adjacent rooms. It is also probable that there is a lot of empty wall space and you could easily use it to hang a collection of prints. Are there areas that you could use to create extra storage space or redefine for another purpose? The space under the stairs, for example, might be used to house a desk or utilised as a laundry. These are all details that will enhance the look and functionality of your hall.

Give plenty of thought to your staircase. What seems to be an immovable feature can be replaced or dressed up according to your budget. Accepting that wood is the material that most of us will inherit when we move into our home, it's a revelation when you think about the other materials that can be used to construct a staircase:

Want to bring more light into the space? Choose a glass balustrade and beach wood treads.

Want to continue an open plan theme? Commission a hanging wire system where the treads are seemingly suspended in space.

Do you live in an industrial-style loft? Add rubber treads to the edge of each step.

Want to be decorative but can't afford a runner (and they can be pricey)? Then leave the central half of each step in natural wood and paint the quarter each side to match the balustrade.

Modernising an old building? Cover the steps with flexible zinc sheeting.

If you take the time to pay attention to your hallway you'll be rewarded with a welcome every time.

49. Upwardly mobile

Climbers are one of the most versatile groups of plants going, perfect for climbing over arches, rambling through trees and shrubs, and masking ugly buildings and blank walls.

They're also great for softening hard edges throughout the garden. But despite their wanderlust and tearaway reputation, climbers also need a certain degree of TLC. Indulge their foibles and their fads with careful planting, regular food and water, and the correct pruning, and the social climbers of the plant world will pay you back with a stunning array of colours.

The best border in the world can be ruined by a backdrop of rotting fence panels, garage roof or uninspiring wall. Enter those rampant runners like Russian vine whose sprays of snowy white flowers can cloak a shed overnight. Ivy is another garden staple, yet often overlooked for more exotic climbing cousins. But with foliage that ranges from dark green to bright gold, and berries that veer from black to cream, it can clamber over anything from tree stumps to outhouses, adding a verdant and mystical air as it goes.

Virginia creeper is another well-known and energetic climber, much loved for its magnificent autumn colour. Well worth growing too is the Crimson Glory Vine, its large plate-sized leaves also turning a brilliant red in autumn. Slightly less invasive are the honeysuckle, rambling rose and jasmine. Try the purple and cream flowered honeysuckle (Lonicera periclymenum) or the evergreen honeysuckle (Lonicera japonica 'Halliana'). Both have a delicious, subtle perfume. Rosa banksiae 'Lutea', with its masses of small yellow flowers is vigorous and needs a strong structure – preferably a tree – to attack. R. felicité perpetué has clusters of creamy pink flowers and at 3.5m is more easily controlled. The climbing rose, Albertine, grows easily but within reason, with salmon buds opening to pale pink.

At the turn of the year there's nothing so welcoming as the brave, bright yellow flowers of the winter flowering jasmine (Jasmine nudiflorum). The white flowered version (Jasmine officinale), given a little shelter, will also romp away and scent the air in summer. Clematis need to be pruned at the right time in order to encourage flowers. Read the label carefully.

50. Work that colour

Colour scheming your whole house may sound like a huge challenge but by breaking it down room by room it is simply a matter of application.

Stick with colours from the same broad family spectrum across most of your home or at least introduce the same colour in some form or another in each room. But there are three alternatives for successful colour scheming so take your pick from the list below. And if you decide to break the rules in the odd space (hopefully just the box room) then you can live with your own guilt.

Take a look at a colour wheel and consider adopting the red and orangey siblings. Move around the wheel and introduce yourself to the yellow and greens or opt for the blues and purples. Each of these groups can affect your mood and effect changes of perception of the shape and size of the room. At the most basic level, for example, a red dining room will stimulate, a yellow dinning room will cheer you up, and a blue room will engender a sense of calm.

The size of rooms should have an influence on your colour choices. If you have a series of small rooms you'll need to stick to a lighter palette. Where there's the luxury of generous proportions you can afford to move to the darker colours in the spectrum.

Here are your choices:

Tonal scheme: This is where you pick just one colour but use it in varying tones. With purples, for example, you might combine the palest lavender and lilac, magenta, plum and wine. For greens, you might use eau de nil, olive, sage and pine.

Harmonious scheme: Choose colours that are closely associated. The best way to do this is to look at a rack of paint charts and take three or four adjacent to each other. Start with red, next to it you'll find terracotta, copper and then chestnut.

Complementary scheme: This uses colours that are opposites of each other. Orange versus blue, green versus scarlet, yellow versus purple. You will need to decide which one of the two colours will be more dominant in a room; indecision here can cause infighting that will wreck the scheme.

51. Pests

How can green gardeners protect their crops?

Whilst spraying roses with washing-up liquid and picking off caterpillars may be effective, it is time-consuming, and a range of biological predators is now available that will thrive in the warm conditions of a greenhouse or conservatory.

You can buy small vials of parasitic wasps, ladybird larvae and other tiny bugs to let loose on your pest-infested vegetation. The whitefly, for instance, destroys tomatoes and peppers by leaving a sticky trail that attracts sooty moulds. But a tiny wasp called Encarsia formosa lays its eggs inside the immature whitefly, killing them at the same time. Red spider mites suck the sap from a variety of plants, causing them to wilt, but they can be defeated by the introduction of another predatory mite, Phytoseiulus. In the same way you can introduce Aphidius and Aphidoletes into your greenhouse or conservatory to control aphids.

Vine weevils are among the most destructive of pests. While the adult beetles will nibble at leaves, it's the grubs that do the real damage, devouring the roots until the plant dies. But help is at hand in the form of a pathogenic nematode that can be watered into the soil to attack the milky white grubs.

Nematodes are also available to take on chafer grubs, leatherjackets and slugs. These biological controls are largely sold through mail order from the Internet, and to be effective you need to use them at exactly the correct time. But they are harmless to humans, pets and other wildlife.

There's little mistaking another destructive creature, the lily beetle, with its bright red body and black legs (the Cardinal beetle has the same colourings but is twice as big). Both the adult and grub feed on the leaves and flowers of lilies and fritillaries, and while they are one of those pests that are best picked off and destroyed, go carefully as the bugs are prone to simply drop off the leaves into the undergrowth as soon as they sense you coming. Lily beetles also overwinter as adults, so if you grow lilies in pots it pays to have a good rummage in the compost to hunt any out.

Add to these controls the likes of companion planting, encouraging more wildlife into your garden, making sure your plants aren't congested, and crop rotation, and suddenly the chemical-free gardener doesn't feel quite so alone.

52. You've got the look

If you're happy to work with some guidelines in place, you'll reap the rewards in terms of creating an appealing and desirable space. It's all about putting together the furniture, soft furnishings and accessories that match a certain mood.

Think about spaces that you are drawn to. These could be a good indication of your personal style. If you find yourself drawn to grand stately homes or always book a cosy country cottage for your holidays, these could be a starting point for tailoring a room to suit. Use a mood board to help you put together the look, incorporating a picture of your ideal room to inspire you as you work.

It's the lavish use of fabrics and ornate detailing that set a stately home style. Consider long draping curtains complete with decorative pelmets and tasselled tiebacks. In the lounge you can look for a sofa that includes piles of cushions in its design. For the bedroom choose a four-poster bed or a design with a scrolling iron headboard and decorative posts finished with balls or finials. If you are drawn to this kind of place you'll be happy to fill the room with lots of extra furniture and accessories. Bring in a pouffe or covered footstool, a nest of tables and a writing desk complete with matching chair. Include one or two rugs on the floor to augment the 'soft' look of the room.

Taste in music? You might worship at the feet of Elvis and so employ a retro approach to your interior.

Love of gardening? Cultivate a collection of floral prints that will give a theme for your scheme.

An historical period? Look for reproduction – or if you have the bank balance original – antique furniture.

Another country? Source sumptuous silks from the Orient, porcelain painted in China or hand-carved accessories from Indonesia.

This should be polarising your thoughts. So now consider the practicalities of putting your plan into action. What about structural alterations? Will knocking two rooms into one give you the space you need to make a dramatic statement? Will your style work in the space that you have? Light-drenched loft style is difficult to achieve in a basement flat.

If you set a style and get all the elements right, then you'll be happy to live with the look for years.

brilliant ideas

This book is published by Infinite Ideas, creators of the acclaimed **52 Brilliant Ideas** series. If you found this book helpful, here are some other titles in the **Brilliant Little Ideas** series which you may also find interesting.

- **Be incredibly healthy:** 52 brilliant little ideas to look and feel fantastic
- **Enjoy great sleep:** 52 brilliant little ideas for bedtime bliss
- **Find your dream job:** 52 brilliant little ideas for total career success
- **Get fit:** 52 brilliant little ideas to win at the gym
- **Get rid of your gut:** 52 brilliant little ideas for a sensational six pack
- **Quit smoking for good:** 52 brilliant little ideas to kick the habit
- **Relax:** 52 brilliant little ideas to chill out
- **Rescue our world:** 52 brilliant little ideas to save the planet
- **Seduce anyone:** 52 brilliant little ideas for being incredibly sexy
- **Shape up your life:** 52 brilliant little ideas for becoming the person you want to be
- **The laid back wine guide:** 52 brilliant little ideas for free-thinking drinking
- **Win at winter sports:** 52 brilliant little ideas for skiing and snowboarding

For more detailed information on these books and others published by Infinite Ideas please visit www.infideas.com.

See reverse for order form.

Qty	Title	RRP
	Be incredibly creative	£4.99
	Enjoy great sleep	£5.99
	Find your dream job	£5.99
	Get fit	£5.99
	Get rid of your gut	£4.99
	Quit smoking for good	£4.99
	Relax	£5.99
	Rescue our world	£4.99
	Seduce anyone	£5.99
	Shape up your life	£5.99
	The laid back wine guide	£4.99
	Win at winter sports	£4.99
	Add £2.49 postage per delivery address	
	TOTAL	

Name: ....

Delivery address: ....

....

....

E-mail:............................Tel (in case of problems): ....

By post Fill in all relevant details, cut out or copy this page and send along with a cheque made payable to Infinite Ideas. Send to: *Brilliant Little Ideas*, Infinite Ideas, 36 St Giles, Oxford OX1 3LD. **Credit card orders over the telephone** Call +44 (0) 1865 514 888. Lines are open 9am to 5pm Monday to Friday.

Please note that no payment will be processed until your order has been dispatched. Goods are dispatched through Royal Mail within 14 working days, when in stock. We never forward personal details on to third parties or bombard you with junk mail. The prices quoted are for UK and RoI residents only. If you are outside these areas please contact us for postage and packing rates. Any questions or comments please contact us on 01865 514 888 or email info@infideas.com.